think big

Compiled by Dan Zadra
Designed by Steve Potter and Jenica Wilkie

COM·PEN´·DI·UM™
Publishing

ACKNOWLEDGEMENTS

These quotations were gathered lovingly but unscientifically over several years and/or contributed by many friends or acquaintances. Some arrived—and survived in our files—on scraps of paper and may therefore be imperfectly worded or attributed. To the authors, contributors and original sources, our thanks, and where appropriate, our apologies. —The editors

WITH SPECIAL THANKS TO

Jason Aldrich, Gerry Baird, Jay Baird, Justi Baumgardt, Neil Beaton, Doug Cruickshank, Jim Darragh, Kari Cassidy-Diercks, Kyle Diercks, Josie and Rob Estes, Jennifer Hurwitz, Dick Kamm, Liam Lavery,Connie McMartin, Janet Potter & Family, Diane Roger, Cristal Spurr, Sam Sundquist, Roger von Oech, Heidi Wills, Kobi Yamada, Robert & Val Yamada, Tote Yamada, Anne Zadra, and August & Arline Zadra

CREDITS

Compiled by Dan Zadra
Designed by Steve Potter and Jenica Wilkie

ISBN: 1-932319-08-5

Printed in China

CHOOSE TO LIVE, WORK AND SUCCEED IN THE MOST POWERFUL NATION ON EARTH: IMAGINATION.

—DAN ZADRA

Nothing energizes an organization faster or better than a big idea. In their landmark book, *Built to Last*, James Collins and Jerry Porras analyzed 1,700 years of successful corporate track records, including modern-day blue-chippers such FedEx, Disney, Motorola, IBM etc. One conclusion:

"Visionary companies may appear strait-laced to outsiders, but they're not afraid to make bold commitments to Big Hairy Audacious Goals (BHAGS). Like climbing a mountain or going to the moon, a BHAG may be daunting and perhaps risky, but the adventure, excitement, and challenge of it grabs people in the gut, gets their juices flowing, and creates immense forward momentum."

Albert Einstein was a big thinker and so was Mother Teresa. But you don't have to be a genius or a saint to come up with breakthrough ideas that blow the doors off the competition. You and every person in your company or community can do it, not just now and then, but all the time. For starters, just think of something that would be "wonderful" if it were only "possible". Then set out together to make it possible. Here in these pages are some inspiring insights and reminders to get you going.

In every organization there are always certain people who are designated as "creative types." The truth is, we are all creative types; we all have unique perspectives and insights that we can and must contribute to the greater good. As every great company has already realized, the gradual accumulation of a lot of little ideas from everyone isn't little.

Think big!

Dan Zadra

The brain is a mass cranial nerve tis

Robert Half You are Nature's great

of making and storing enough cor

TAKE OUT YOUR
ON IT— IT GETS

total number would be expressed

miles of zeros. We're talking about

molecules of your body are the same

nebulae, that burn inside the stars

Victor Tenbaum Imagine the possibi

sue, most of it in mint condition.
est miracle. Your brain is capable
nections and information that the

RAIN AND JUMP
ALL CAKED UP. —Mark Twain

by a one, followed by 6.5 million
your brain here! Don Ward The
molecules that make up the
themselves. We are star stuff.
ities. Think! Thomas Watson, IBM

YOU HAVE TO T
SO WHY NOT

Fortune favors the bold. **Terance** It
that we do not dare; it is because
difficult. **Seneca** One of the greatest
question: "If I could do anything I
no object—what would I do?" In m
have the luxury of asking that ques
there is still time, to have a magnif
Who dares nothing need hope for

HINK ANYWAY, THINK BIG?

—Donald Trump

is not because things are difficult

we do not dare that things are

freedoms is being able to ask the

wanted with my life—money being

ny parts of the world, people don't

:ion. **M. Burnett** I dare you, while

:ent obsession. **William Danforth**

nothing. **T. Von Schiller**

BIG IDEAS ARE SO HARD TO RECOGNIZE, SO FRAGILE, SO EASY TO KILL. DON'T FORGET THAT, ALL OF YOU WHO DON'T HAVE THEM.

—John Elliot, Jr., Ogilvy & Mather

New ideas are like loaves of bread. They often emerge from the oven looking half-baked, homely and lumpy. Give them a chance to rise. Chic Thompson A new idea is delicate. It can be killed by a sneer or a yawn; it can be stabbed to death by a joke or worried to death by a frown on the right person's brow. Charles Brower Form the habit of saying "Yes" to a good idea. Then list all the reasons why it will work. There will always be plenty of people to tell you why it won't work. Gil Atkinson

All new ideas pass through three st[ages]
they are violently opposed. Third, t[he]
Arthur Schopenhauer If the commo[n]
that one can fall off the edge, then i[t]
the horizon and discover a new world
in Columbus is not his having disco[vered]
search for it on the faith of his ow[n]
you, then they laugh at you, then they
Gandhi Today's shocks are tomorrow[s]

**DON'T WORRY, THE NE[XT]
UNDERSTAND YOU. TH[E]
TO TRY TO CONVI[NCE]**

ges. First, they are ridiculed. Second, ey are accepted as being self-evident. y held belief is that the world is flat, s clearly impossible to sail beyond Cherie Carter-Scott What I admire ered a world, but his having gone to opinion. Turgot First they ignore ight you, then you win. Mohandas K. s conventions. Carolyn Heilbrun

KT GENERATION WILL E REAL CHALLENGE IS CE YOUR PEERS. —Frank Vizzare

Discontent is the first necessity of
Status-quo seekers are so busy
longer see "what can be." Unknown
Raymond Loewy, Designer If it ain't

CONTENTMI
SMOTHER OF

faster. Take smart; make it smart
Cigna Advertisement Don't be afraid
pedestal. Dan Zadra Learn to say
"yes" to the great. John Mason

progress. Thomas Edison

protecting "what is" that they no

Never leave well enough alone.

broke, fix it. Take fast; make it

ENT IS THE
INVENTION.

—Ethel Mumford

er. Take good; make it great.

to knock your best ideas off the

"no" to the good, so you can say

IF YOU CAN'T WRITE YOUR IDEA ON THE BACK OF A BUSINESS CARD, YOU DON'T HAVE AN IDEA.

—David Belasco

The ability to succinctly express an idea is virtually as important as the idea itself. Bernard Baruch Coca-Cola's 1898 two-word marketing plan: "Bottle it." Sears Roebuck's 1902 six-word catalog marketing strategy: "Satisfaction guaranteed, or your money back." Avis Rent-A-Car's three-word marketing positioning statement: "We try harder." Apple Computer's initial six-word Vision statement: "A personal computer on every desk." Great Ideas

THE MOON COU[LD BE]
SHINING IF IT PAI[NED]
THE LITTLE DOGS

Accept it: You will be criticized this[...]
Maybe even in an hour. Karen Salm[...]
critics. They play no ball, they fight[...]
because they attempt nothing. Gen[...]
deal with the flyweights of the world[...]
in thwarting you at every turn. Suc[...]
you, so what? If people agree with[...]
Do just once what others say you[...]
attention to their limitations again[...]

LD NOT GO ON
 ATTENTION TO
THAT BARK AT IT.

—Anonymous

year. Maybe even this week.
ansohn The galleries are full of
no fights. They make no mistakes
David M. Shoup It never pays to
They take far too much pleasure
Grafton If people don't agree with
you, so what? Dr. Robert Anthony
can't, and you will never pay
Edmund Brown, Jr.

SUCCESS FOUR FLIGHTS THURSDAY MORNING ALL AGAINST TWENTY-ONE MILE WIND STARTED FROM LEVEL WITH ENGINE POWER ALONE AVERAGE SPEED THROUGH AIR THIRTY-ONE MILES LONGEST 59 SECONDS INFORM PRESS HOME CHRISTMAS.

—Orville and Wilbur Wright (Telegram to their father from Kitty Hawk, North Carolina, Dec. 17, 1903)

Flight by machines heavier than air is insignificant, if not utterly impossible. Simon Newcomb, 1902 Everything that can be invented has been invented. Charles H. Duell, 1911 In the future, computers will likely weigh far less than 1.5 tons. Popular Mechanics, 1949 Who the hell wants to hear actors talk? H.M. Warner, Founder of Warner Brothers, 1927 I think there is a world market for maybe five computers. Thomas Watson, 1960's

When we die and go to heaven, our
you discover the cure for such and
be asked at that precious moment is
Wiesel You are the one and only you

WE ARE ALL BOI
WHY IS IT SO MANY

you are going to do in appreciation
you can answer. Dan Zadra Change
she is, not when she tries to become
You have to play a long time to be a

Maker is not going to say, why didn't
such? The only thing we're going to
why didn't you become you? Elie
that ever was or ever will be. What

N ORIGINALS—
OF US DIE COPIES?

—Edward Young

of this miracle is a question only
occurs when one becomes what
what she is not. Ruth P. Freedman
ble to play like yourself. Miles Davis

A possibility was born the day you w[ere] live. **Marcus Solero** There is more in[side] to see it, perhaps, for the rest of ou[r] for less. **Kurt Hahn** I read and walke[d] searching endlessly for someone wo[rth] darkness and change my life. It neve[r] could be me. **Anna Quindlen** The in[side] moment to sacrifice what we are fo[r] **Du Bos** All the wonders you seek ar[e]

PEOPLE BECOME
EVEN BEETHOVEN B

e born and it will live as long as you

us than we know. If we can be made

ives, we will be unwilling to settle

or miles at night along the beach,

erful who would step out of the

crossed my mind that that person

ortant thing is this: to be able at any

what we could become. **Charles**

within yourself. **Sir Thomas Brown**

WHO THEY ARE.
CAME BEETHOVEN.

—Randy Newman

PEOPLE WHO AI
THEIR LAURELS
THEM ON THE

Asked which of his works he would
tect Frank Lloyd Wright at age 83 r
Let's build a future—not just polish
is the death of possibilities. James
only opens out into wider horizons
you to explore. Barbara Sher We res
ocean calling in our dreams, and we
fill our sails once more to test the s

E RESTING ON ARE WEARING WRONG END.

—Malcolm Kushner

select as his masterpiece, archi-
plied, "My next one." Michael Nolan
the past. Frank Vizzare Complacency
Mapes Each destination you reach
new and undiscovered countries for
here while we can, but we hear the
know by the morning, the wind will
ams. Tome Kimmeri & Michael Lille

WARNING: DATES IN CALENDAR ARE CLOSER THAN THEY APPEAR.

—Bumpersticker

Begin doing what you want to do now. We are not living in eternity. We have only this moment, sparkling like a star in our hand—and melting like a snowflake. **Marie Beynon Ray** If we wait until we've satisfied all the uncertainties, it may be too late. **Lee Iacocca** It is astonishing how short a time it takes for very wonderful things to happen. **F. Burnett** It's amazing how fast doors open to us when we dare to take control. **Catherine Ponder**

Gutenberg connected the coin pu[nch] the printing press. Mendel connec[ted] genetics. Fred Smith connected the[...] wheel to create Federal Express'[...] The roll-on deodorant was modele[d...] movies inspired drive-in banks. The[...] design for the billion-dollar Velcr[o...] connect—use it! **Roger von Oech**

CONCEPTION
OF CONN

ch with the wine press to create
d math with biology to create
hub and spoke idea of the wagon
overnight distribution plan.
after the ballpoint pen. Drive-in
common cocklebur inspired the
ndustry. You have the power to

S A MATTER
ECTION. —Dan Zadra

Whenever I see everyone rushing in
think about moving the other way
else zigs, zag. **Tom Yobaggy** *People*
applying the "opposites" approach

THINK SI

more words than pictures, so we'l
Most magazines show glamorous
ordinary people in ordinary ways—
Barbara Walters washing dishes, o
the lottery." **Great Ideas** Don't follow

one direction, I know it's time to

Armand Hammer When everyone

Magazine was conceived by

as in: "Most magazines have

DEWAYS.

—Edward de Bono

have more pictures than words.

people in glamorous ways, or

so let's do the opposite. We'll show

an unemployed dishwasher winning

trends, start trends. **Frank Capra**

EVERY NOW AND THEN, BITE OFF MORE THAN YOU CAN CHEW.

—Kobi Yamada

You cannot be wimpy out there on the dream-seeking trail. Dare to break through barriers, to find your own path. **Les Brown** In each of us are places where we have never gone. Only by pressing the limits do you ever find them. **Dr. Joyce Brothers** I am always doing things I can't do—that's how I get to do them. **Pablo Picasso** Getting into trouble is our genius and glory. **John Pfeiffer** Either you decide to stay in the shallow end of the pool or you go out in the ocean. **Christopher Reeve**

WHAT ISN
WON'T

Most of the things worth doing in the
before they were done. Louis D. Bra
wouldn't have done the experiment
that said you can't do this. Spencer
one-hundred assertions that a thing
unwillingness to do it. William Feath
capacity. Ella Wheeler Wilcox Reach
one thought could be opened. Life

T TRIED, WORK.

—Claude McDonald

world were said to be impossible

ndeis If I had thought about it, I

The literature was full of examples

Silver Behind ninety-nine out of

cannot be done is nothing, but the

r Trust in your own untried

ut and open the door that no

s behind it. Kelly Ann Rothaus

I learned that inspiration does not a
kinetic, energetic, striving, but it con
the time. **Brenda Ueland** Thousands
brains every day. Some are pure ger
least long enough to write them down
the city of your comfort and go into
What you'll discover will be wonde
Alan Alda Follow the tugs that come
one gets these gentle urges and sho
sound absolutely insane, they may b

SOMETIMES YO
TO TRUST YOU

ways come like a bolt, nor is it
es into us slowly and quietly and all
of perceptions race through our
us. Give them the red light for at
Ralph M. Ford You have to leave
the wilderness of your intuition.
ul. What you'll discover is yourself.
from the heart. I think that every-
uld listen to them. Even if they
worth going with. Victoria Moran

OU JUST HAVE
UR INTUITION.

—Bill Gates, Microsoft

WHOEVER INVENTED THE FIRST WHEEL WAS SMART. THE GUY WHO INVENTED THE OTHER THREE WAS A GENIUS.

—Sid Caesar

Most new discoveries are suddenly-seen things that were always there. **Susanne K. Langer** To see what is in front of one's nose requires a constant struggle. **George Orwell** The more original a discovery, the more obvious it seems afterward. **Arthur Koestler** Did you know that left shoes and right shoes were invented less than 200 hundred years ago? **Great Ideas** Creative thinking may simply mean the realization that there's no particular virtue in doing things the way you have always done them. **Rudolph Flesch**

CREATIVITY IS ALL
TO MAKE MISTAKES
WHICH ONE

If you haven't made any mistakes
thing wrong. **Susan Jeffers** Errors
James Joyce Most of my advances
what is when you get rid of what
architect's most useful tools are an
a wrecking bar at the site. **Frank**
a sort of creeping common sense
the only things one never regrets

OWING YOURSELF

ART IS KNOWING

S TO KEEP. —Scott Adams

ately, you must be doing some-
are the portals of discovery.
were by mistake. You uncover
sn't. **Buckminster Fuller** An
eraser at the drafting board, and
.loyd Wright Most people die of
and discover when it is too late that
are one's mistakes. Oscar Wilde

The best way to have a good idea is
Treat ideas as though they were baby
water. Only a handful will survive, but
the average employee submits no mo

YOU HAVE TO KISS
TO FIND A

his or her company. Imagine if every
down one idea, large or small, every
result would be a torrent of ideas and
and bewilder your most aggressive

o have lots of ideas. **Dr. Linus Pauling**

ish. Throw thousands out into the

hat is plenty. **Unknown** Each year

e than two ideas for improvement to

A LOT OF FROGS
PRINCE.

—3M Innovation Team

erson in your company wrote

day for the next six months. The

mprovements that would challenge

competitors. **Michael Nolan**

PEOPLE DON'T GIVE A HOOT
ABOUT WHO MADE THE ORIGINAL
WHATZIT.
THEY WANT TO KNOW
WHO MAKES THE
BEST ONE.

—Howard M. Newton

Lots of very successful people know a good thing the minute the other guy sees it first. **J.E. Hedges** I start where the last person left off. Most of my ideas belonged to other people who didn't bother to develop them. My principle business is giving commercial value to the brilliant but misdirected ideas of others. **Thomas Edison** I never think about why something hasn't been done already—but why nobody has done it right. **Marcia Kilgore**

Often what we're looking for leads us
better. Think of the times you've g
ular book, and then found something
behind you. **Roger von Oech** Penic
electric current, saccharin, the micro
Post-It Notes were all fortuitous by-
else. **Hirsch Goldberg** Every exit is
ber that Columbus was looking for
Stoppard In every problem or se
lent or greater benefit—if you will o

SUCCESS IS OFTEN TH
A MISSTEP IN THE

o something much different and
e to a library in search of a partic-
even better and juicier on the shelf
n, X rays, rubber, photography,
wave oven, even Silly Putty and
products of looking for something
an entry somewhere else. Remem-
ndia when he found America. **Tom**
back there is the seed of an equiva-
y stop to look for it. **Bob Moawad**

E RESULT OF TAKING
IGHT DIRECTION.

—Al Bernstein

THUNDER IS
BUT IT IS LIGHTNING T

When I hear about people making
productive work or contributing any
"How do I get in on that?" **Dave Barry**
who has got to the top without hard
the top, but it should get you pretty
sit down to work because I am inspi
sit down to work. **Oscar Hammerstein**
ing. People who are successful at
work goes with it, so they are surpris

MPRESSIVE, IAT DOES THE WORK. —Mark Twain

vast fortunes without doing any
hing to society, my reaction is,
The truth is, I do not know anyone
work. It will not always get you to
hear. **Margaret Thatcher** I do not
ed; I become inspired because I
You always feel you are not deserv-
what they do know what kind of
ed at the praise. **Virginia Hamilton**

Never tell a young person that something cannot be done. God may have waited centuries for someone ignorant enough of the impossible to do that very thing. **J.R. Holmes** The wise are instructed by reason; ordinary minds by experience; the stupid, by necessity; and brutes by instinct. Children are remarkable for their intelligence and ardor, for their curiosity, their intolerance of shams, the clarity and ruthlessness of their vision. Men of genius are often dull and inert in society, as a blazing meteor, when it descends to earth, is only a stone. A child miseducated is a child lost. The voice of parents is the voice of gods, for to their children they are heaven's lieutenants. A child is a quicksilver fountain spilling over with tomorrows and tomorrows and that is why she is richer than you and I; and that is why she will inherit the earth. Men and nature must work hand in hand. The throwing out of balance of the resources of nature throws out of balance also the lives of men. be prudent, and therefore they attend

IF I RAN THE WORLD BIGGER PRIZES IN

generation after generation. **Pearl S. Buck** Children's talent to endure stems from their ignorance of alternatives. The soul is healed by being with children. A child is a beam of sunlight from the Infinite and Eternal, with possibilities of virtue and vice, but as yet unstained. When I approach a child, he inspires in me two sentiments: tenderness for what he is, and respect for what he may become. **Louis Pasteur** The fundamental magic of flying, a miracle that has nothing to do with any of its practical purposes—purposes of speed, accessibility, and convenience—and will not change as they change. Let us put our minds together and see what life we can make for our children. Every child is an artist. The problem is how to remain an artist once he grows up. We worry about what a child will become tomorrow, yet we forget that he is someone today. We can educate our children in what no one knew yesterday, and prepare in our schools for what no one knows yet, but some must know tomorrow. Teach the children to dream with open eyes.

hing cannot be done. God may
gnorant enough of the impossible
he young do not know enough to
ot the impossible, and achieve it,

LD, I WOULD PUT
CEREAL BOXES.

—Rachel McCullough,
Age 9

Buck When I approach a child, he
erness for what he is, and respect
eur We are now where we must
knew yesterday, and prepare our
Margaret Mead We must teach our
Harry Edwards

THERE WILL BE THOSE WHO WILL TELL YOU THAT YOU CAN'T MAKE IT BECAUSE OF WHERE YOU LIVE, BECAUSE OF HOW YOU LOOK, BECAUSE OF THE WAY YOU TALK. WE ALL HAVE HEARD THAT—I ALMOST LISTENED.

—L. Douglas Wilder

Credentials are not the same as accomplishments. **Robert Half** It's not your blue blood, your pedigree, or your college degree. It's what you do with your life that counts. **Millard Fuller** It doesn't interest me where or what or with whom you have studied. I want to know what sustains you, from the inside, when all else falls away. **Oriah Mountain Dreamer** I do what I love. You don't need an MBA to be successful. You need a unique concept and guts. **Deborah Karabin**

You and I know that there is a co
the screwball. So suffer the screv
While some may see them as the
Because the people who are crazy
the world, are the ones who do.

BE NICE TO MISFIT
THEIR IDEA IS PAY

Trust your crazy ideas. **Dan Zadra**
wants you to "be realistic, quit dro
head out of the clouds and your feet
prosper, steadfastly ignore that adv

elation between the creative and

all gladly. **Kingman Brewster, Jr.**

crazy ones, we see genius.

enough to think they can change

Think Different" Apple Computer Ad**

S. CHANCES ARE,

NG YOUR SALARY.

—Harold Geneen

Caution! The left-brained world

ming, be more like us, get your

on the ground." To advance and

ce. **Marilyn Grey**

DON'T JUST CREATE WHAT TH
CREATE WHAT IT

The entrepreneur finds a need and fills
creates a need and fills it. **Denis E.**
ask people to tell me what they want
moves them until it moves them. **Miles**
thing. No customer asked for electric
make electricity so cheap that only
Thomas Edison Henry Ford articula
still largely a network of horse trails
multitude. It will be so low in price
be unable to own one—and enjoy with
pleasure in God's great open spaces

MARKET NEEDS OR WANTS. WOULD LOVE. —Josh Armstrong

t. The innovator anticipates or

Waitley When I write music, I don't

to hear. They don't really know what

Davis The customer generates no-

ights. **W. Edwards Deming** I shall

the rich can afford to burn candles.

d his vision when the nation was

We will build a motor car for the great

that no man making a good wage will

his family the blessing of hours of

Building Community

This seems to be the law of progress

a spiral rather than a perpendicular

of the way, and yet it turns out that

the time. **Frances E. Willard** There

LAW OF ACCUMULATI
OF A LOT OF LITTLE

Welch I don't believe in one big pro

build on a series of wins. It's like

long term is really just a bunch of

Lappos Arrange whatever pieces

n everything we do; it moves along

we seem to be actually going out

we were really moving upward all

s no straight line to a dream. **Jack**

ON: THE SUM TOTAL HINGS ISN'T LITTLE.

—Dan Zadra

ect or silver bullet; you have to

LEGO blocks. **Niraj Patel The**

short terms taped together. **Nick**

come your way. **Virginia Woolf**

IF YOU HAVE A COMPANY WITH AN ITSY-BITSY VISION, YOU HAVE AN ITSY-BITSY COMPANY.

—Anita Roddick

Great companies make meaning. **Richard Pascale** A company should stand for something, fulfill a purpose, and contribute something useful—hopefully something special, even wonderful—or it shouldn't bother being a company. **Dan Zadra** Leaders and followers are both following the invisible leader—the big idea, their shared purpose. **Don Ward** It isn't common ground that bonds people together, it's higher ground. **Tom Brown**

On your journey to your new goal, trip alone. **Rhonda Abrams** You can everything. **David Allen** The secret team. **John Wooden** Every organiza the people who come up with new catchers, too. These are the people implement the great idea. **John Ho** imagine, other people can make r you leave off and everybody else be

LITTLE PEOPLE
BIG PEOPLE S

you don't have to make the
do anything—but you can't do
to stardom is the rest of the
tion needs pitchers. These are
deas. Every organization needs
who champion the charge to
mes, Jr. Anything one person can
al. **Jules Verne** Figure out where
gins. **George McCabee**

KEEP SECRETS.
HARE IDEAS.

—Phil Rognier

BIG COMPANIE
COMPANIES THAT
STAND TOGETHEI

Ideas bring people together, but

Meyer When your organization oper

be knocked out by one punch. **Mike**

young tigers who believe anything

lieutenants who are old enough to

Give me some old warriors who wil

Give me men who can listen and

who can listen and learn from men

and a ship—and we will reinvent the

S ARE SMALL AND TOGETHER, AND SUCCEED.

—Jeff Goforth

deals hold them together. **Bill**

tes like a strong family, you can't

Krzyzewski God, give me some

s possible. Give me some solid

ead but young enough to dream.

speak up for our cherished ideals.

earn from women; and women

Give us a mapmaker, a compass,

world. **Hannibal's Redux**

The lure of quantity is the most dan
row, who will really care how fast we
know what we are building with ou
is easy; measuring better is hard.

QUALITY IS A
SOARING

ful when I look around and can't fin
I do. **Lois Wyse** We knew we love
time we did, we made people happy
Fields In the end, beautiful things

gerous of all. **Simone Weil** Tomor-

grew? Isn't it more important to

growth, and why? Measuring more

Ron Kendrick I think I'll be sucess-

PROUD AND
THING.

—Jessica Julian

nyone who does it better than

naking great cookies and every

That was our business plan. **Debbi**

nake money. **Geoffrey Beene**

SOMETIMES I GET TO PLACES JUST WHEN GOD'S READY TO HAVE SOMEBODY CLICK THE SHUTTER.

—Ansel Adams, Photographer

The nature of all work is to be well prepared for a good accident. **Sydney Lumet** Some opportunities arrive in their own mysterious hour, on their own terms and not yours, to be seized or relinquished forever. **Gail Godwin** To every person there comes that special moment when he is tapped on the shoulder to do a very special thing unique to him. What a tragedy if that moment finds him unprepared for the work that would be his finest hour. **Winston Churchill**

The most damaging phrase in the

been done that way." **Rear Admira**

thing for the human soul when it fi

Charlotte P. Gilman Do not become

Van Gogh I have an almost comp

faith in the possibility of something

how things always have been done.

I cannot afford the luxury of a clo

might improve the past. **Clara Bar**

are frightened of new ideas. I'm fr

The good old days? The only good

NOSTALGIA IS A

English language is: "It's always

Grace Hopper It will be a great

ally stops worshipping backwards.

he slave of your model. Vincent

te disregard of precedent and a

better. It irritates me to be told

I defy the tyranny of precedent.

ed mind. I go for anything new that

on I can't understand why people

ghtened of the old ones. John Cage

days are ahead. Alice Childress

SEDUCTIVE LIAR.

—George Ball

What one has to do usually can be

esting to note that when the Allies

HAVE FAITH. WHEN
HAVE TO LAND THAT PL
RUNWAY—EVEN IF YOU C.

formula for synthetic rubber (so lo

on their drawing boards. **Dr. Larry**

is possible. **G.A. Borghese** All things

beings realize that everything is a

know what you want, and you want

find ways to get it. **Jim Rohn**

done. **Eleanor Roosevelt** It's inter-

ran out of rubber during WWII, the

**YOU ABSOLUTELY
NE, THERE WILL BE A
N'T SEE IT SOMETIMES.**

—John Hamm

g a mystery) quickly materialized

Case It is necessary; therefore, it

are possible once enough human

stake. **Norman Cousins** When you

t badly enough, you can always

And have you touched a life? And ha[ve]
wanted to be? And have you told the[m]
dance? **Unknown** Do not let your fire
spark, in the hopeless swamps of the
not-yet, the not-at-all. Do not let the

WHAT IF THE RES[T]
WAS THE BEST

frustration for the life you deserved[.]
Check your road and the nature o[f]
can be won. It exists, it is real, it is

ve you become what you always

moon that you would love the next

go out, spark by irreplaceable

approximate, the not-quite, the

hero in your soul perish, in lonely

T OF YOUR LIFE

OF YOUR LIFE?

—Alfred Lord Tennyson

out have never been able to reach.

your battle. The world you desired

possible, it is yours. Ayn Rand

I believe that the creativity that twisted
put erasers on pencils is great enough
peace. **Wilfred Peterson** Somewhere

IT'S EASY TO MAKE A BU

MAKE A DI

tion to each of the world's problems
we can build a more hopeful world.
the solutions in society will come from
south. They will come from islands
people with integrity who want to do

a piece of wire into a paperclip and
to create brotherhood and universal
on this planet, someone has a solu-

K, BUT IT'S TOUGH TO
FERENCE.

—Tom Brokaw

t might be one of us. With your help,
Marianne Larned I don't believe that
the left or the right or the north or the
within those organizations, islands of
something. Karl-Henrick Robert

Don't waste too much of the time you
creating a life we can look forward to
Make some piece of the world care
of the sun, think of your life as jus
but relish small pleasures. H. Jackson
God at the end of my life, I would h
bit of talent left, and could say "I us
Bombeck Live all you can; it's a mis
is sending back good wishes and wa

COULD IT BE
THE BEST

have left. Thinking big means
looking back on. Diane Branson
Robert B. Horton With every rising
begun. Unknown Think big thoughts
Brown, Jr. When I stand before
e that I would not have a single
d everything you gave me." Erma
ake not to. Henry James The future
ting with open arms. Kobi Yamada

YOU SAVED
OR LAST?

—Last Chance Cafe

This book may be ordered
directly from the publisher, but
please try your local bookstore first!
Call us toll free at 800-91-I$_4$D$_3$E$_3$A$_2$S$_7$ or come
see our full line of inspiring products at
www.compendiuminc.com

COM·PEN·DI·UM™
Publishing

$\mathcal{E}$nriching the lives of millions, one person at a time.™